From Seed to
JACK·O'·LANTERN

Lothrop, Lee & Shepard Company · New York

From Seed to
JACK·O'·LANTERN

Hannah Lyons Johnson

photographs by Daniel Dorn

Library of Congress Cataloging in Publication Data

Johnson, Hannah Lyons.
    From seed to jack-o'-lantern.

SUMMARY: Text and photographs introduce the growing cycle of the pumpkin from the planting
of the seed until the fruit is ripe and ready for use.
    1. Pumpkin—Juvenile literature. [1. Pumpkin] I. Dorn, Daniel, illus. II. Title.
SB347.J63   635'.62   74-6458
ISBN 0-688-41644-6   ISBN 0-688-51644-0 (lib. bdg.)

For our inquisitive sprout, Dylan

Books by Hannah Lyons Johnson
with photographs by Daniel Dorn, Jr.

Picture the Past: 1900-1915
Let's Make Jam
From Seed to Jack-O'-Lantern
Let's Bake Bread
Let's Make Soup
From Apple Seed to Applesauce

By Hannah Lyons Johnson
with illustrations by Tony Chen

Hello, Small Sparrow

This is Gary Laurino and his grandfather, Edward Laurino, Sr., farmers of Laurino's Farm, Shrewsbury, New Jersey. Special thanks to them and to Mr. W. B. Johnson, one of Rutgers University's vegetable specialists.

Spring's flat pumpkin seeds
unfolding from earth
to be
fall's jack-o'-lanterns.

In the shortening days of late summer when teachers welcome children back to their classrooms and the morning air is shivery, pumpkins start appearing. They are for sale in supermarkets and at roadside stands and can be seen squatting on porches and sitting in windows all over America. They make people think about Halloween and Thanksgiving. Pumpkins are a symbol of fall's harvest and the bounty it brings. These pumpkins began on farms, and their growing started way back in springtime when people were thinking of baseball and tulips and being outside without coats.

Some time in May or June when the earth is warm and no longer soggy from spring rains, the farmer prepares his field for planting. Using a tractor to pull the plow, he first turns the earth over.

He then makes it smooth and level.

Carrying a cloth sack filled with pumpkin seeds, the farmer then begins to plant by hand.

He walks across the field in a straight line. Every three to five feet he kicks a hole in the soil with the heel of his boot, throws a few seeds into the hole, and uses his boot to cover them with soil. He plants the seeds in straight rows, leaving the spaces between the rows wide and even until the whole field is planted.

With the help of warm sunlight and moisture in the earth, the seeds germinate or sprout in eight to ten days. They break through the crust of earth and open out a set of two seed leaves. The pumpkin plants are born!

Every day the plants grow a little bigger.

seed leaves

true pumpkin leaf

Soon a different type of leaf appears on the stems. The two seed leaves feed the plants until they develop other leaves for making food. Then the seed leaves dry up and fall off. The plants begin to spread out and soon develop two different kinds of flower buds.

Some of the buds are on long stems. These will become male flowers.

Still other buds appear on short stems and sit on top of green bulbous knobs. These will become female flowers. The bulbous knobs are called ovaries and will grow into pumpkins, but only with some help from bees!

The male flower contains tiny yellow grains called pollen. This pollen is carried from the male flower to the female flower by bees.

The farmer sets up hives of bees, usually squash bees, right in the pumpkin field. The pumpkin flowers bloom at night and early morning, but close up during the heat of the day. The bees are attracted by the flowers' sweet nectar and yellow color. They use the nectar to make their honey. So the plants and the bees need one another.

While collecting the nectar from inside the blossoms, the bees brush up against the rod-like stamen in the center of the male flower. The stamen is covered with pollen grains which are brushed off on the bees' hairy bodies and legs.

stamen with pollen grains

When the bees buzz into female flowers, the pollen grains are knocked off the bees' bodies and are trapped on the sticky stigma deep in the center of the flower. This is called *pollination*. Each pollen grain grows down through the flower into the ovary. Inside the ovary the grain joins with a tiny ovule and becomes a pumpkin seed. This process is called *fertilization*. The flowers gradually dry up and drop off the pumpkins after pollination and fertilization have taken place.

The spreading pumpkin plants are often called vines. Weeding is done with a plow attachment called a cultivator, which turns the soil over between the plants so weeds can't get started growing. Weeds take food and moisture from the soil that is needed by the growing pumpkin plants. During the hot summer days of July and August, the vines creep across and over the rows and spaces between them until the field is a mass of tangled leaves and flowers and growing green pumpkins. At this time, cultivating (weeding) is no longer possible.

As the days go by, the pumpkins grow larger and larger. The pumpkin plants need just the right amount of rain and sun. Too much rain and the plants will rot on the ground. Too much sun and they will dry up and the growing pumpkins will get ripe too soon before Halloween.

About 120 days after the planting of the seeds, the pumpkins are ripe. (Since they contain seeds, they are fruits.) They have grown plump and turned from green to deep yellow and orange. Some have bumps and lumps and speckles on them. Some are very round and others are long. Some are very large and others are small. Pumpkins, like people, come in all shapes, sizes, and hues.

When ripe, the pumpkins' tough stems are cut and the pumpkins are left in the field.

Walking through the field to find a pumpkin with just the right shape, size, and color is an adventure for many people. From miles around, people come to buy them.

Some of them were children when they chose their first farm fresh pumpkin, and now bring their own children to the same farm in September or October.

The pumpkin treasures are carried carefully home to be used whole as decorations, carved out to become jack-o'-lanterns, or cut up for use in pumpkin pies, bread, custard, and in other favorite recipes.

A carefully carved out pumpkin can be a jolly or fear-some creature. You may want to draw a face on the pump-kin so you will have a carving guide.

Always carve in a direction away from you to avoid cutting yourself. If you put a candle inside, a small holder will help it stand up steadily—or you can carve out a hole in the bottom of the pumpkin for the candle to stand in.

Instead of throwing away the seeds from inside your jack-o'-lantern, try roasting and eating them.

Here's how to do it:

Crunchy Roasted Pumpkin Seeds

—Wash the stringy matter off of the seeds under cold water.

—Blot the seeds dry between paper towels.

—Spread the seeds out on a cookie sheet so they are in a single layer and not touching each other.

—Sprinkle the seeds with salt and put them in a preheated 350° oven. (Ask an adult to help you with the oven!)

—Roast the seeds for ½ to 1 hour and check them often.

—They are done when dry and light brown.*

—Let cool before eating.

*Cooking time will depend on the size and wetness of the seeds.

If you want to grow some pumpkins for next Halloween, save a few unroasted seeds in an envelope until next spring. When the ground outside is warm and soft, kick a hole in the soil you have turned over and made smooth and plant your saved seeds. If you don't have much room in your yard for a spreading pumpkin vine, or if you have no yard at all to plant one in, there is a type of pumpkin plant that grows more like a bush and can even be grown in a very big pot. It's called the Cinderella Pumpkin. Seeds can be ordered from Joseph Harris Company, Moreton Farm, Rochester, N.Y. 14624. Each plant should produce two pumpkin fruit about ten inches in diameter. If you grow one inside, you will have to collect pollen from the male flower and sprinkle it inside the female flower yourself. (You could use a small paintbrush for this.) That way, you can be a bee! However you plant, you can watch the exciting and wonderful way that nature gives its pumpkin presents to you!

ABOUT THE AUTHOR

Hannah Lyons Johnson is the author of Lothrop's highly popular *Let's Bake Bread* and *Hello, Small Sparrow*. She is a former elementary schoolteacher whose interests include baking, handicrafts, and literature. Mrs. Johnson also enjoys organic gardening and it was this interest which prompted her to write *From Seed to Jack-o'-Lantern*. Mrs. Johnson lives in New Jersey with her husband and two young sons.

ABOUT THE PHOTOGRAPHER

Daniel Dorn is a self-employed professional photographer who especially enjoys photographing children. He also took the pictures for Mrs. Johnson's *Let's Bake Bread*. Mr. Dorn lives in New Jersey with his wife and two young daughters.